BIOLOGY Field Notes

Be a CHICKEN Expert

by
Noah Leatherland

BEARPORT
PUBLISHING

Minneapolis, Minnesota

Credits

All images are courtesy of Shutterstock.com, unless otherwise specified. With thanks to Getty Images, Thinkstock Photo, and iStockphoto.

Recurring – MoonRock, Milano M, Colorlife, Life of Trickster, vectorplus, The_Pixel. Doctor Character throughout – NotionPic. Cover – Olhastock, Krivosheev Vitaly. 4–5 – Marie Charouzova, Nattapong Nakcharin. 6–7 – Niselwitch, Matauw. 8–9 – Miroslav Hlavko, Maria G. Murphy. 10–11 – tea maeklong, Bob Pool, lifelikeafrog. 12–13 – Nadezhda Kharitonova, Sunil_Sharma_ab. 14–15 – ChaniDAP, Dovzhykov Andriy. 16–17 – eurobanks, Bennian, Roman Kybus. 18–19 – Groomee, Mayukh Karmakar. 20–21 – Fotikphoto, New Africa, Jan Mleziva, FarHorizonFarm. 22–23 – tristan tan, Majna.

Bearport Publishing Company Product Development Team

President: Jen Jenson; Director of Product Development: Spencer Brinker; Managing Editor: Allison Juda; Associate Editor: Naomi Reich; Associate Editor: Tiana Tran; Art Director: Colin O'Dea; Designer: Kim Jones; Designer: Kayla Eggert; Product Development Assistant: Owen Hamlin

Library of Congress Cataloging-in-Publication Data is available at www.loc.gov or upon request from the publisher.

ISBN: 979-8-88916-964-2 (hardcover)
ISBN: 979-8-89232-483-0 (paperback)
ISBN: 979-8-89232-119-8 (ebook)

© 2025 BookLife Publishing
This edition is published by arrangement with BookLife Publishing.

North American adaptations © 2025 Bearport Publishing Company. All rights reserved. No part of this publication may be reproduced in whole or in part, stored in any retrieval system, or transmitted in any form or by any means, electronic, mechanical, photocopying, recording, or otherwise, without written permission from the publisher. Bearport Publishing is a division of Chrysalis Education Group.

For more information, write to Bearport Publishing, 5357 Penn Avenue South, Minneapolis, MN 55419.

CONTENTS

Meet the Biologist............4
A Chicken's Body 6
Scratch and Peck 8
Head to Tail.................10
Cozy Homes 12
Can Chickens Fly?...........14
Dinnertime 16
Clucking and Squawking 18
Life Cycle..................20
Cool Chickens...............22
Glossary....................24
Index.......................24

MEET THE BIOLOGIST

Hello! My name is Dr. Helen Cooper, and I am a **biologist**. I have traveled the world to learn all about chickens. They are amazing birds!

Being a chicken **expert** is a lot of work. I filled this notebook with everything I know about chickens. Will you read it? Together, we can find out even more!

A CHICKEN'S BODY

There are so many cool things about chickens! They have eyes on the sides of their heads. This helps them keep watch for **predators** while pecking at food.

Chickens can see more colors than humans.

Chickens have red flaps of skin on the top of their heads called a comb. A red wattle hangs from their throats. This bright skin helps chickens cool down when they get too hot and warms them up when they are cold.

Comb

Wattle

SCRATCH AND PECK

Chickens have sharp, clawed feet. They use them to scratch and dig for food. A pointy spike called a spur comes out of the side of each foot, too. Chickens use their spurs to fight and to keep themselves safe from predators.

Spurs

Male chickens are called roosters. **Female** chickens are called hens.

Nostril

As chickens grow, so do their beaks.

Beaks help chickens in many different ways. They use their beaks to eat, build nests, keep themselves safe, and clean their feathers. Chickens can also smell through the nostrils on their beaks.

HEAD TO TAIL

Feathers help chickens in many ways. They keep chickens warm and dry. Feathers also keep chickens from being bitten by insects. Some feathers help chickens **camouflage** themselves to blend in with the colors of their homes.

How many chickens do you see?

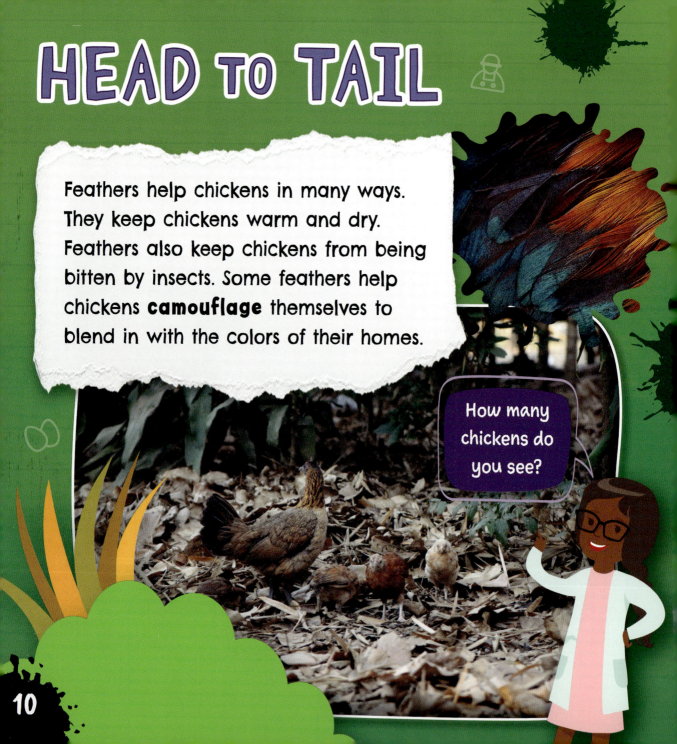

Molting starts at the head and finishes at the tail.

Every year, chickens go through a process called molting. This is when chickens lose old feathers to make room for new ones to grow. It usually happens before winter, so chickens will have new feathers for colder weather.

COZY HOMES

Most chickens are **domestic** animals that live on farms. But there are wild chickens called jungle fowl. They live in **habitats** with lots of trees, such as forests.

A female jungle fowl

A male jungle fowl

Coops are little buildings farmers make for their chickens.

Both domestic chickens and jungle fowl set up cozy nest homes. Many domestic chickens make their nests in coops. Jungle fowl gather grass and sticks to build this place to rest.

CAN CHICKENS FLY?

Many birds can fly. However, most chickens' wings are not big enough to let them take flight for a long time. Some domestic chickens can only fly short distances.

All birds have **hollow** bones, which makes it easier for them to get off the ground.

The feathers on a chicken's wings are long and stiff. This helps them lift off when they flap their wings.

DINNERTIME

Chickens are **omnivores**. While they often eat grasses and seeds, they also feed on any insects that they find. People who raise domestic chickens on farms give them chicken feed, too.

Jungle fowl hunt snakes, mice, and lizards. They use their sharp claws and pointy beaks to grab the moving meal.

CLUCKING AND SQUAWKING

Chickens are noisy birds. They make lots of different clucking and squawking sounds. They do this to **communicate**. Clucking in different ways tells other chickens different things.

When a rooster makes a loud call, the sound is called a crow.

Roosters are known for their *cock-a-doodle-doo* calls. This sound is a message to other chickens. It says, "Back off!" Roosters make this call to say they are in charge.

LIFE CYCLE

Chicken life cycles start with hens laying their eggs in nests. They sit on their eggs to keep them warm. Soon, baby chickens called chicks hatch out of these eggs.

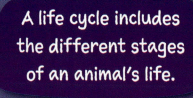

A life cycle includes the different stages of an animal's life.

A chick

A juvenile chicken

An adult chicken

As chicks get bigger and bigger, so do their feathers. When chicks are about 10 weeks old, they are called juveniles. By about 18 weeks, they are adults and are ready to lay eggs.

Most chickens can live for up to eight years.

COOL CHICKENS

From their powerful beaks to their sharp claws, chickens are so cool! I hope you've enjoyed learning about these amazing birds.

You have just begun your chicken adventure. There is so much more to learn about them. Continue to study. Soon, you'll be an expert, too!

GLOSSARY

biologist a person who studies and knows a lot about living things

camouflage a covering or coloring that makes animals look like their surroundings

communicate to share information

domestic raised and tamed for use by humans

expert someone who knows a lot about a subject

female a chicken that can lay eggs

habitats places in the wild where animals normally live

hollow with an empty space inside

male a chicken that cannot lay eggs

omnivores animals that eat both plants and animals

predators animals that hunt other animals for food

INDEX

beaks 9, 17, 22
chicks 20–21
claws 8, 17, 22
eggs 20–21
feathers 9–11, 15, 21
hens 8, 20

jungle fowl 12–13, 17
juvenile 21
nests 9, 13, 20
predators 6, 8
roosters 8, 19
wings 14–15